SPOTLIGHTS

ROCKS
AND MINERALS

Written by Neil Curtis

OXFORD UNIVERSITY PRESS

ACKNOWLEDGMENTS

Illustrated by
The Maltings Partnership, Debra Woodward

Picture credits
Front Cover TL SPL/Michael Barnett; **CL** SPL/Martin Land;
CR SPL/Roberto de Gugliemo; **CB** SPL/Martin Land,
Back Cover G.R. Roberts; **9** GSF; **11** GSF/Dr. Basil Booth;
12 SPL/Jan Hinsch; **22** GSF/Dr. Basil Booth; **26** TIB/Romilly Lockyer

GSF   Geoscience Features, Kent, UK
SPL   Science Photo Library, London, UK
TIB   The Image Bank, London, UK

Published in 1998 by
Oxford University Press
198 Madison Avenue
New York, New York 10016

Devised and produced by
Andromeda Oxford Limited
11-15 The Vineyard
Abingdon
Oxfordshire OX14 3PX
England

Copyright © 1993 Andromeda Oxford Limited
Reprinted 1999

Library of Congress Cataloging-in-Publication Data
Curtis, Neil.
    Rocks and minerals / written by Neil Curtis.
        p.   cm. — (Spotlights)
    Originally published: Hemel Hempstead, Hertfordshire : Simon &
    Schuster Young Books, 1993.
    Includes index.
    ISBN 0-19-521392-0
    1. Rocks—Juvenile literature.   2. Minerals—Juvenile literature.
[1. Rocks. 2. Minerals.]   I. Title.   II. Series.
QE432.2.C87   1998
552—dc21
                                                97-19687
                                                    CIP
                                                     AC

Printed in Italy by Vallardi, Milan

CONTENTS

INTRODUCTION

The planet Earth was formed some 4.5 billion years ago. Its skin, the crust on which we walk, is made of rocks. The rocks, in turn, are composed of minerals. And even the very heart of the earth — the mantle and core — are made of rocky material. Finding out more about rocks and minerals can be fun, and you are also learning about the world on which you have evolved. We make use of rocks and minerals in many ways, too. And rocks and minerals are often beautiful, so they can be fascinating to collect.

PROTECTING THE PLANET

All over the world, there are sites that have attracted rock and mineral collectors. Some of them have been badly damaged by careless collecting. Do not just hammer wildly at the rocks. Make sure you have permission to collect, and only remove a small specimen without harming the rest of the area.

HOW TO USE THIS BOOK

This book explores and explains the world of rocks and minerals. The book begins with a look at the structure of the earth and the ways in which minerals are formed. It then goes on to explain in more detail the three main types of rocks and the ways in which they have been used.

INTRODUCTION

Concise yet highly informative, this text introduces the reader to the topics shown. This broad coverage is complemented by a more detailed exploration of particular points in the numerous captions.

INSET ART

Aspects of the subject that help to explain particular points are shown in an inset, along with an explanation of their significance.

SPOTLIGHTS

A series of illustrations at the bottom of each page encourages the reader to look out for easy-to-find or typical rocks and minerals that can be found in museums or in the countryside.

VOLCANO

A volcano is an o[...] earth's crust throug[...] rock (lava), gas, ste[...] other material break[...] the surface. The con[...] ash around the openi[...] called a volcano. Volc[...] eruptions can be very [...] causing widespread de[...] but they also provide i[...] information about the s[...] the earth. Volcanoes are [...] regions where there is a [...] flow of heat from the ma[...] as the "Ring of Fire" aro[...] Pacific Ocean.

DIFFERENT KINDS OF VOLCANO[...]

Volcanoes erupt in different ways [...] and spew out different products. F[...] example, they may be explosive or [...]

fissure   Hawaiian   vulcanian

LOOK OUT FOR THESE

☐ PAHOEHOE
This is a kind of la[...] that cascades slowl[...] downslope. When i[...] cools, it has a smooth, ropy-looki[...] surface.

18

6

HEADING
The subject matter of each spread is clearly identified by a heading prominently displayed in the top left-hand corner.

DETAILED INFORMATION
From the formation of volcanoes to meteorites from outer space, the reader is given a wealth of information to help him or her appreciate the world of rocks and minerals.

ILLUSTRATIONS
High quality, full-color art brings this exciting look at rocks and minerals to life. Each spread is packed with visual information.

REFERENCE TAB
Each group of subjects is keyed with a special color to the contents page of the book so that different sections can be found quickly and easily.

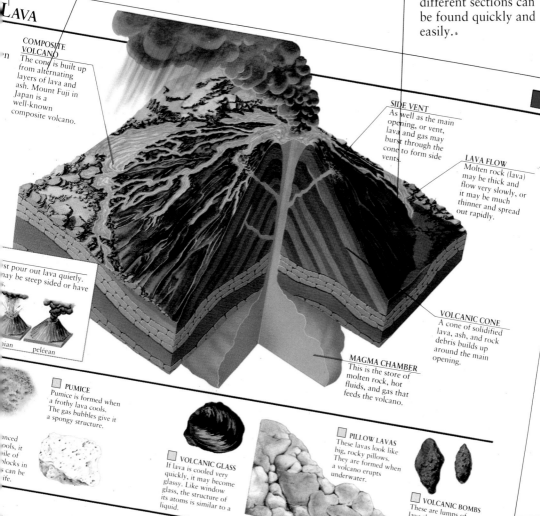

LAVA

COMPOSITE VOLCANO
The cone is built up from alternating layers of lava and ash. Mount Fuji in Japan is a well-known composite volcano.

st pour out lava quietly. nay be steep sided or have

nian   peléean

SIDE VENT
As well as the main opening, or vent, lava and gas may burst through the cone to form side vents.

LAVA FLOW
Molten rock (lava) may be thick and flow very slowly, or it may be much thinner and spread out rapidly.

VOLCANIC CONE
A cone of solidified lava, ash, and rock debris builds up around the main opening.

MAGMA CHAMBER
This is the store of molten rock, hot fluids, and gas that feeds the volcano.

PUMICE
Pumice is formed when a frothy lava cools. The gas bubbles give it a spongy structure.

VOLCANIC GLASS
If lava is cooled very quickly, it may become glassy. Like window glass, the structure of its atoms is similar to a liquid.

PILLOW LAVAS
These lavas look like big, rocky pillows. They are formed when a volcano erupts underwater.

VOLCANIC BOMBS
These are lumps of lava that have been thrown from a volcano. They take on rounded shapes as they fly through the

WHAT IS THE EARTH'S CRUST MADE OF?

The earth is not made of the same material all the way through. It is made up of different layers. The thin outer layer that forms the continents and ocean floors is called the crust. It is made of rock. Pebbles on the beach are rocks, and the hard stone blocks of a cliff or quarry face are rocks. There are many different kinds of rocks. In general, though, a rock is a mass of substances called minerals.

There are three types of rock. Igneous rock is formed when hot, molten rock (liquid rock, called magma) cools down. Sedimentary rocks are often made up of fragments of other rocks. Metamorphic rocks are formed from other rocks that are changed by heat or pressure.

KINDS OF CRUST
The crust under the ocean is thinner than that under the continents. The continental crust is like granite. The oceanic crust is made of basalt.

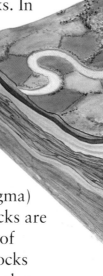

continental crust

LOOK OUT FOR THESE

 **GRANITE**
Granite is an igneous rock. It is usually a mottled gray, pink, or white color. The grains of minerals are large.

 **BASALT**
Basalt is blackish in color. It is a fine-grained igneous rock because the lava from which it was formed cooled very quickly.

SANDSTONE
Sandstone is a sedimentary rock. The grains of the rocks from which it is made are big enough to be seen with the naked eye.

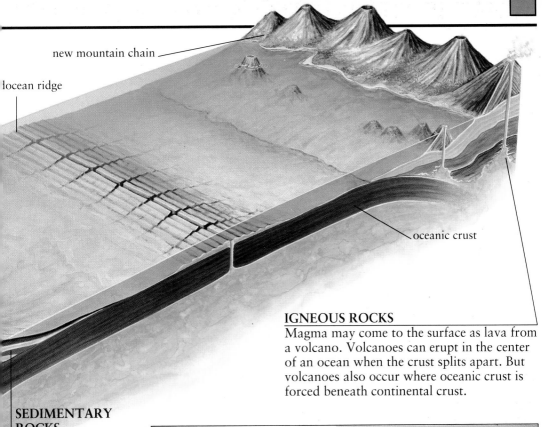

new mountain chain

ocean ridge

oceanic crust

IGNEOUS ROCKS

Magma may come to the surface as lava from a volcano. Volcanoes can erupt in the center of an ocean when the crust splits apart. But volcanoes also occur where oceanic crust is forced beneath continental crust.

SEDIMENTARY ROCKS

Rocks are broken down by the weather. The debris (sediment) is often carried to the sea by rivers. Later, layers of sediment may harden into rock.

OUTCROPS OF GRANITE

Granite cools and hardens deep in the crust. When granite is exposed by erosion, it often forms bold and distinctive outcrops.

CHALK

Chalk is a special kind of sedimentary rock. It is made from the skeletons of tiny sea creatures.

SCHIST

Schist is a metamorphic rock. It has been changed by heat and pressure. It has a flaky, banded, and sometimes shiny look.

MARBLE

Marble is a limestone that has been changed mainly by heat. It is often white in color but may be streaked with different colors.

9

WHAT IS A MINERAL?

A rock is a mass of minerals. Minerals occur naturally and each mineral has a definite chemical composition. They can be made up of an individual chemical element, such as gold. Often, they are compounds; for example, the mineral calcite is a compound of the chemical elements calcium, carbon, and oxygen. Usually, minerals are formed as crystals. Most rocks are made up of the so-called rock-forming minerals.

DIKE
A dike is a wall-like body of rock. Magma has cut across the layers of the surrounding rock. Dikes are often made of the igneous rock syenite.

feldspar
biotite
hornblende
quartz

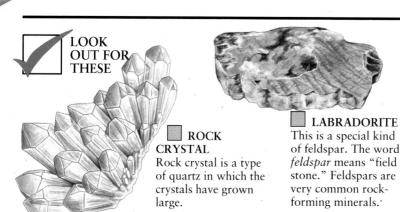

PARTS OF A ROCK
Granite is coarse grained. It is made from crystals of the minerals feldspar, biotite, pyroxene, and quartz.

LOOK OUT FOR THESE

ROCK CRYSTAL
Rock crystal is a type of quartz in which the crystals have grown large.

LABRADORITE
This is a special kind of feldspar. The word *feldspar* means "field stone." Feldspars are very common rock-forming minerals.

HORNBLENDE
This greenish- or blackish-colored mineral is found in many igneous and metamorphic rocks.

GEODE
A geode is a hollow stone in which near-perfect crystals of minerals, such as quartz, have grown.

OLIVINE
Olive green in color, olivine is found in basalts and other dark rocks, such as gabbro.

AUGITE
Augite is usually dark green or black. It is found in some rocks changed by heat and in dark igneous rocks, such as basalt.

BIOTITE
Biotite is a black, brown, or greenish mineral that often occurs in flaky layers. It is found in granites and metamorphic rocks.

HOW CAN YOU IDENTIFY MINERALS?

In rocks where the individual grains are very large, the minerals can often be identified using only a small magnifier, called a hand lens, and a few other simple pieces of equipment.

For more accurate identification, a scientist grinds a piece of the rock into a sliver so thin that it is almost transparent. Then the rock can be examined under a microscope, using a special kind of light (polarized light) that shows the individual mineral crystals.

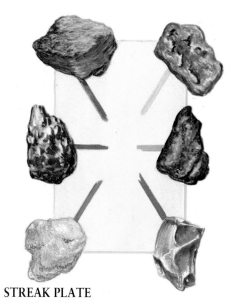

IN CLOSE-UP

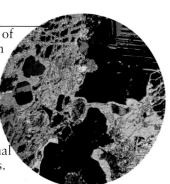

This thin sliver of olivine has been photographed through a microscope using polarized light. You can see the individual mineral crystals.

STREAK PLATE

The color of an opaque, metallic-looking mineral in a powdered form — its streak — can help to identify it. You get this by scratching a piece on a porcelain streak plate.

DENSITY

You can get a rough idea of the density of a mineral by holding a piece of it in your hand to test if it feels heavy or light.

HARDNESS

The hardness of a mineral can be tested by trying to scratch it with simple objects or other minerals.

LOOK OUT FOR THESE

PYRITE

In good specimens, pyrite (fool's gold) can be recognized by its cube-shaped crystals and its shiny gold color. Pyrite has a greenish-black streak.

CALCITE

These shapes are called rhombs. Calcite always breaks, or cleaves, into such fragments.

QUARTZ

When quartz breaks, or fractures, the surface of the break may be ridged, like a seashell.

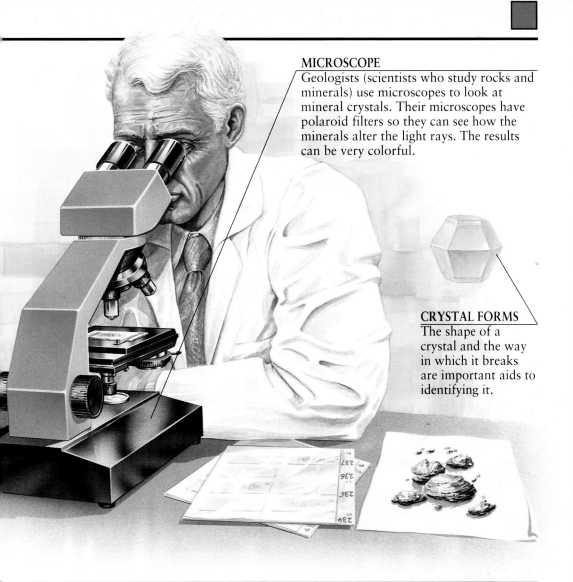

MICROSCOPE

Geologists (scientists who study rocks and minerals) use microscopes to look at mineral crystals. Their microscopes have polaroid filters so they can see how the minerals alter the light rays. The results can be very colorful.

CRYSTAL FORMS

The shape of a crystal and the way in which it breaks are important aids to identifying it.

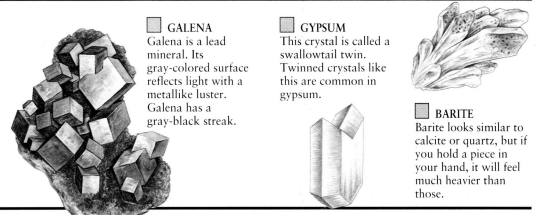

GALENA

Galena is a lead mineral. Its gray-colored surface reflects light with a metallike luster. Galena has a gray-black streak.

GYPSUM

This crystal is called a swallowtail twin. Twinned crystals like this are common in gypsum.

BARITE

Barite looks similar to calcite or quartz, but if you hold a piece in your hand, it will feel much heavier than those.

WHAT ARE MINERALS MADE FROM?

Every mineral is made from a definite combination, or compound, of chemical elements. A chemical element is a substance, such as carbon, that cannot easily be broken down further because all the atoms from which it is made are the same. There are more than 90 elements that occur naturally in the rocks of the earth or in the atmosphere surrounding our planet. Just 8 of these, however, make up almost 99 percent of all rocks.

THE BIG BANG
About 15 billion years ago, all matter was created in a gigantic explosion.

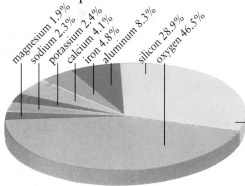

magnesium 1.9% · sodium 2.3% · potassium 2.4% · calcium 4.1% · iron 4.8% · aluminum 8.3% · silicon 28.9% · oxygen 46.5%

ELEMENTS OF THE EARTH'S CRUST
This chart shows the eight main elements found in the earth's crust. Most of the rock-forming minerals are silicates. Silicates contain the elements silicon and oxygen.

LOOK OUT FOR THESE

GARNET
Good crystals of garnet are not uncommon. The crystal form is based on a cube.

CHALCOPYRITE
Chalcopyrite is a copper-iron mineral. It is sometimes called fool's gold like pyrite because of its shiny golden color.

SULFUR
The element sulfur occurs around volcanic craters — for example, in Sicily and Japan. It is used to produce sulfuric acid.

RUBY
Ruby is a gem-quality crystallized mineral, aluminum oxide. Very small amounts of chromium give it its red color.

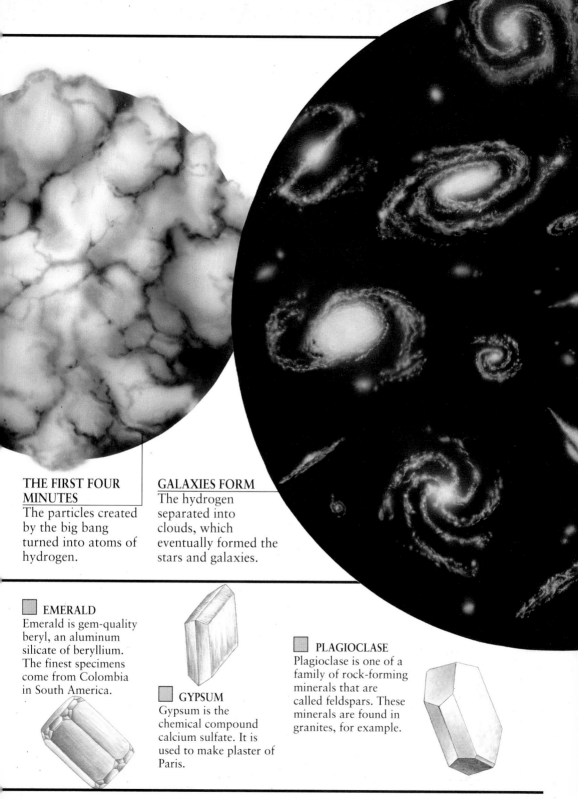

THE FIRST FOUR MINUTES
The particles created by the big bang turned into atoms of hydrogen.

GALAXIES FORM
The hydrogen separated into clouds, which eventually formed the stars and galaxies.

EMERALD
Emerald is gem-quality beryl, an aluminum silicate of beryllium. The finest specimens come from Colombia in South America.

GYPSUM
Gypsum is the chemical compound calcium sulfate. It is used to make plaster of Paris.

PLAGIOCLASE
Plagioclase is one of a family of rock-forming minerals that are called feldspars. These minerals are found in granites, for example.

THE PLANET BENEATH YOUR FEET

Although scientists have been studying worlds beyond our own for centuries, we still know relatively little about the inside of our own planet. In the 1960s, an attempt was made to drill through the earth's crust. The drilling took place in the deep ocean off the west coast of Mexico. Here, the crust was about 3 miles (5 kilometers) thick. However, the attempt was unsuccessful. Nevertheless, we know that the earth consists of three zones: the outer crust, the mantle, and the core. And the core is divided into an inner and an outer zone.

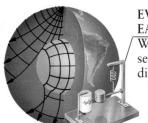

EVIDENCE FROM EARTHQUAKES

When an earthquake occurs, it sends out shock waves in all directions. The waves are affected by the nature of the material through which they travel. Scientists can detect the waves on a seismometer. From the waves they learn more about the inner earth.

 **LOOK OUT FOR THESE**

GRANODIORITE
Granodiorite is similar in composition to the rock that makes up the crust under the continents.

GABBRO
The oceanic crust is made from gabbro and finer-grained basalt. You can find gabbro in sills and dikes.

 **PERIDOTITE**
Scientists believe peridotite is similar to the material from which the mantle is made. It is a dark, heavy rock.

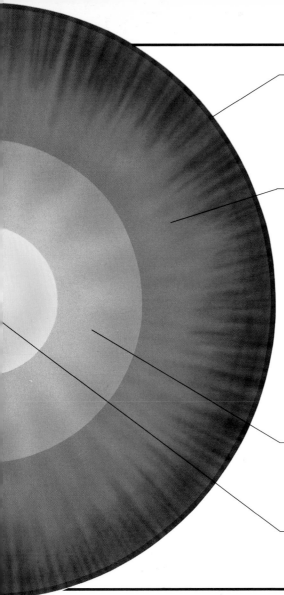

THE CRUST
The outer, rocky crust can be up to 30 miles (50 kilometers) thick under mountain ranges.

THE MANTLE
The mantle reaches a depth of 1,800 miles (2,900 kilometers) and it makes up the bulk of the planet. It is hot and made from a rock composed largely of olivine, called peridotite. In some places mantle material moves very slowly. Magma comes from the mantle.

THE OUTER CORE
This is a very hot, dense liquid made of nickel, iron, and perhaps sulfur.

THE INNER CORE
The inner core is solid and made of nickel and iron.

GLOMAR CHALLENGER
The drilling ship *Glomar Challenger* has been used to drill holes up to 4,920 feet (1,500 meters) deep into the oceanic crust. The ship has taken samples of rocks from the oceanic crust and the sediments that lie on it.

drilling ship

drill

sonar scanners direct drill to the cone of the drill hole

seabed

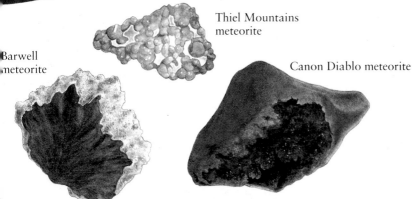

Thiel Mountains meteorite

Barwell meteorite

Canon Diablo meteorite

METEORITES
Meteorites are rocky or metallic fragments that fall to the earth from space. Stony meteorites are the most common kind. The so-called iron meteorites are made of nickel and iron. Their composition is probably similar to the earth's core.

VOLCANOES AND LAVA

A volcano is an opening in the earth's crust through which molten rock (lava), gas, steam, ash, and other material break through to the surface. The cone of lava and ash around the opening is also called a volcano. Volcanic eruptions can be very violent, causing widespread destruction, but they also provide important information about the structure of the earth. Volcanoes are found in regions where there is a greater flow of heat from the mantle, such as the "Ring of Fire" around the Pacific Ocean.

COMPOSITE VOLCANO
The cone is built up from alternating layers of lava and ash. Mount Fuji in Japan is a well-known composite volcano.

DIFFERENT KINDS OF VOLCANOES

Volcanoes erupt in different ways and spew out different products. For example, they may be explosive or they may just pour out lava quietly. The cones may be steep sided or have gentle slopes.

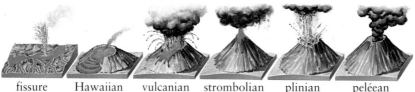

| fissure | Hawaiian | vulcanian | strombolian | plinian | peléean |

LOOK OUT FOR THESE

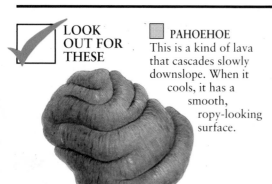

PAHOEHOE
This is a kind of lava that cascades slowly downslope. When it cools, it has a smooth, ropy-looking surface.

AA
As aa (pronounced AH-ah) lava cools, it breaks into a pile of rough, jagged blocks in which the edges can be as sharp as a knife.

PUMICE
Pumice is formed when a frothy lava cools. The gas bubbles give it a spongy structure.

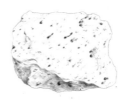

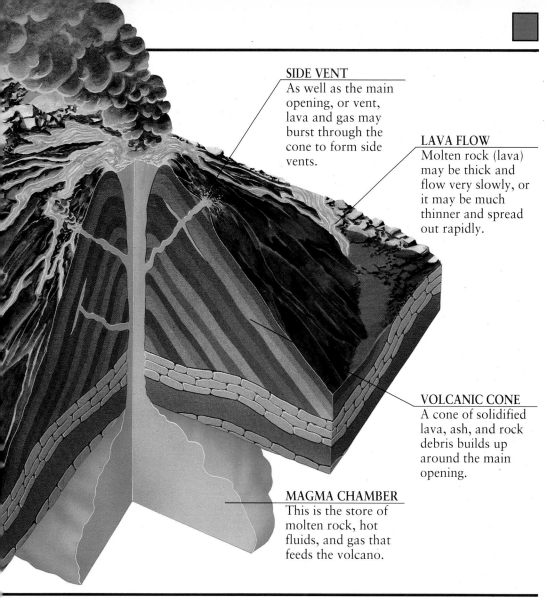

SIDE VENT
As well as the main opening, or vent, lava and gas may burst through the cone to form side vents.

LAVA FLOW
Molten rock (lava) may be thick and flow very slowly, or it may be much thinner and spread out rapidly.

VOLCANIC CONE
A cone of solidified lava, ash, and rock debris builds up around the main opening.

MAGMA CHAMBER
This is the store of molten rock, hot fluids, and gas that feeds the volcano.

■ **VOLCANIC GLASS**
If lava is cooled very quickly, it may become glassy. Like window glass, the structure of its atoms is similar to a liquid.

■ **PILLOW LAVAS**
These lavas look like big, rocky pillows. They are formed when a volcano erupts underwater.

■ **VOLCANIC BOMBS**
These are lumps of lava that have been thrown from a volcano. They take on rounded shapes as they fly through the air.

INTRUDED IGNEOUS ROCKS

Some igneous rocks, such as granite, are coarse grained. They were formed when large bodies of magma cooled slowly within the earth's crust. Sometimes, magma is forced (intruded) into the surrounding rocks as very small bodies. The cooled rock has a medium grain size. The names of the bodies tell you about their shape and the way they relate to the surrounding rocks. In places, they can be seen at the surface where the layers of rock that once covered them have worn away.

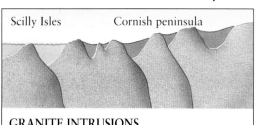

Scilly Isles   Cornish peninsula

GRANITE INTRUSIONS
Dartmoor, Bodmin Moor, St. Austell, Carnmellis, Land's End, and the Scilly Isles in the southwest of England all lie on the exposed tips of granite intrusions.

LOPOLITH AND PHACCOLITH
A lopolith is similar to a sill but it has a sagging, spoon- or saucer-like shape. A phaccolith is lens shaped.

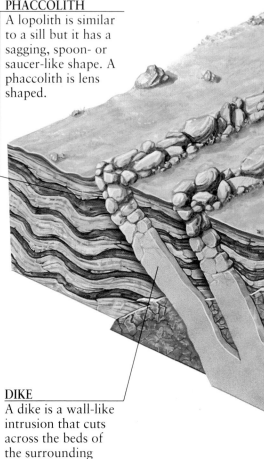

DIKE
A dike is a wall-like intrusion that cuts across the beds of the surrounding rocks. Dikes may be vertical.

 **LOOK OUT FOR THESE**

NEGATIVE DIKE
If a dike is exposed at the surface and is more easily worn away than the rocks around, it resembles a ditch in the rock.

DIORITE
Diorite is a fairly coarse-grained rock. It may be red, pink, white, or gray. It is usually found in dikes, sills, or stocks.

RHYOLITE
Rhyolite is paler and finer grained than diorite. It may occur as a lava flow, and is often banded. Rhyolite is also found in dikes.

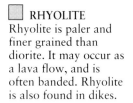

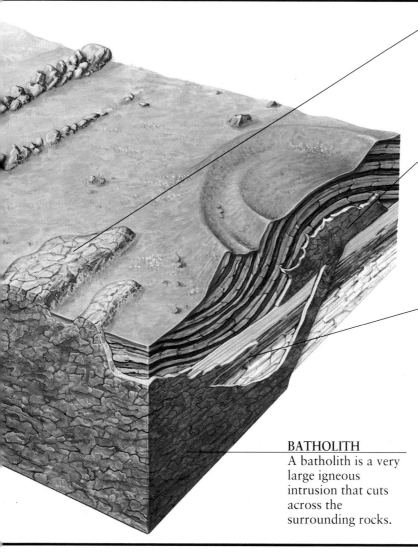

STOCK AND BOSS

A stock is a roughly circular intrusion with steep sides. It is very small. A boss is similar to a stock but larger.

LACCOLITH

A laccolith is similar to a sill but it has a flat floor and domed top.

SILL

A sill consists of igneous rock that has been intruded parallel with the bedding of the surrounding rocks.

BATHOLITH

A batholith is a very large igneous intrusion that cuts across the surrounding rocks.

PEGMATITE

Pegmatite is a very coarse-grained rock. It is found in dikes and veins, often around a granite intrusion. Pegmatites are good sources of ores.

XENOLITH

When magma is intruded into rocks, parts of those rocks may break off and become included in the cooling magma. These are xenoliths.

JOINTING

Joints are splits in igneous rocks that may have been widened and deepened by weathering.

WEATHERING, EROSION, AND DEPOSITION

The temperature and pressure at the earth's surface are very different from those at which rocks form. So when rocks are exposed, they begin to break up. This is called weathering. Heating and cooling cause rocks to crack. Water in joints may freeze, expand, and pry open the rock. The loose material (debris) is carried away by running water, wind, gravity, or moving glaciers. Finally, it is deposited, perhaps in the sea far from its source.

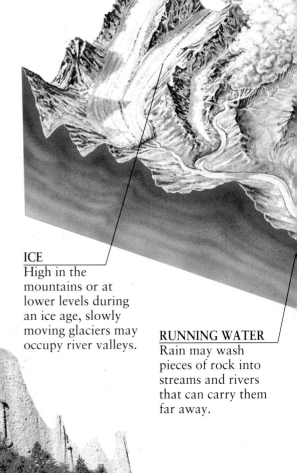

ICE
High in the mountains or at lower levels during an ice age, slowly moving glaciers may occupy river valleys.

EARTH PILLARS
Earth pillars can form if hard boulders protect the ground beneath them and so stop it from being worn away by the rain.

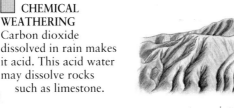

RUNNING WATER
Rain may wash pieces of rock into streams and rivers that can carry them far away.

✓ **LOOK OUT FOR THESE**

■ **FROST-SHATTERED ROCKS**
When water freezes, it expands. This can shatter rocks.

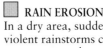

■ **CHEMICAL WEATHERING**
Carbon dioxide dissolved in rain makes it acid. This acid water may dissolve rocks such as limestone.

■ **RAIN EROSION**
In a dry area, sudden violent rainstorms can cause great gashes on soft, sloping ground.

■ **SCREES**
An inland cliff may be weathered so that coarse debris falls to its base. The debris piles against the cliff as a scree slope.

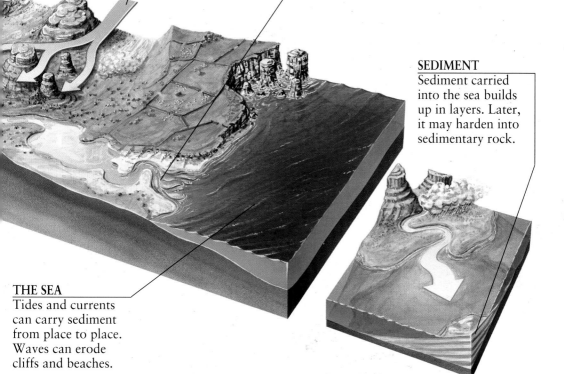

GRAVITY
Loose pieces of rock may simply fall down a slope because of the force of gravity.

WIND
If you have seen a sandstorm or a dust storm, you will know that wind can carry large amounts of fine rock debris.

RIVER DELTA
As the flow of a river slows down as it reaches the sea, a fan-shaped delta of sediment may form.

SEDIMENT
Sediment carried into the sea builds up in layers. Later, it may harden into sedimentary rock.

THE SEA
Tides and currents can carry sediment from place to place. Waves can erode cliffs and beaches.

■ **U-SHAPED VALLEY**
A typical river valley is V-shaped. If it has been scoured by a glacier, it becomes more U-shaped.

■ **SEA STACKS**
When waves crash against cliffs, they erode them and may form an arch. If the roof collapses, a stack is left.

■ **WIND EROSION**
In dry areas, strong winds carrying sand grains can wear away the base of rocks.

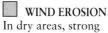

■ **SAND DUNES**
Sand dunes are ripple-like piles of sand built up by the wind. Dunes may be up to 980 feet (300 meters) high.

CONGLOMERATES, SANDSTONES, AND MU

Sedimentary rocks are formed from particles of minerals and other rocks. The particles are deposited in an area, such as the sea, are buried by more layers of sediment, and under pressure are hardened into rock. Over millions of years, the layers of rock may be pushed up out of the sea by movements in the earth's crust.

The particles that make up conglomerates, sandstones, and muds all come from the breakdown of other rocks by weathering and erosion.

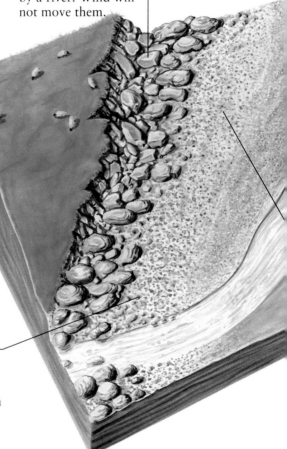

BOULDERS
Large boulders are unlikely to be carried very far by the sea or by a river. Wind will not move them.

PEBBLES
When stones of this size are buried and eventually harden into rocks, they form conglomerates and breccias.

LOOK OUT FOR THESE

CONGLOMERATE
This is a sedimentary rock made from rounded grains that are bigger than 0.08 inch (2 millimeters) in diameter.

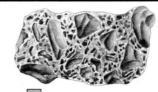

BRECCIA
The angular grains of a breccia have probably been laid down close to their source. During their short journey they have not been rounded.

TILLITE
The sediments in a tillite have been formed and carried by the action of ice rather than water.

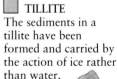

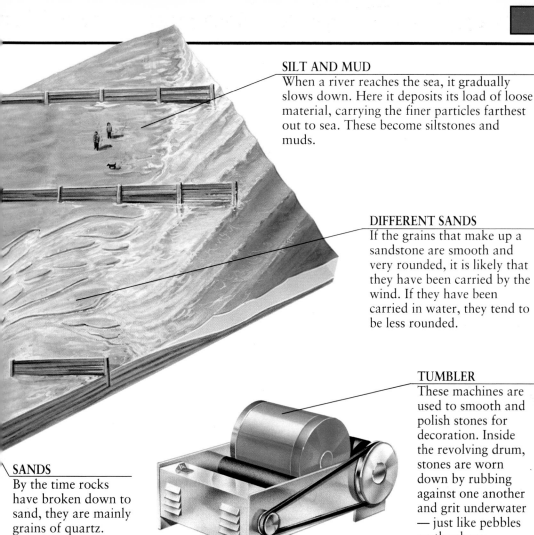

SILT AND MUD

When a river reaches the sea, it gradually slows down. Here it deposits its load of loose material, carrying the finer particles farthest out to sea. These become siltstones and muds.

DIFFERENT SANDS

If the grains that make up a sandstone are smooth and very rounded, it is likely that they have been carried by the wind. If they have been carried in water, they tend to be less rounded.

TUMBLER

These machines are used to smooth and polish stones for decoration. Inside the revolving drum, stones are worn down by rubbing against one another and grit underwater — just like pebbles on the shore.

SANDS

By the time rocks have broken down to sand, they are mainly grains of quartz. Sand in turn becomes sandstone.

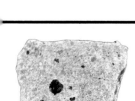

GRIT
Grit is the name given to a sandstone with angular grains. The grains have probably been carried in water.

SANDSTONE
The grains in a sandstone are smaller than 0.08 inch (2 millimeters) in diameter. They may be smooth and round.

BEDDING
Sandstones can show how the beds of sand were originally built up by a current.

direction of current

SHALE
Shale is a sedimentary rock made of silt-sized grains less than 0.0025 inch (0.0625 millimeter) in diameter.

LIMESTONES, FLINTS, AND SALTS

Limestones, flints, and salts are sedimentary rocks, but they are formed in different ways and are made from different substances. At least half of a limestone rock is lime or calcium carbonate. Flint occurs as odd-shaped lumps in chalk and is a type of chert that is made from microscopic crystals of silica. There are different kinds of deposits called salts; the best-known is common salt.

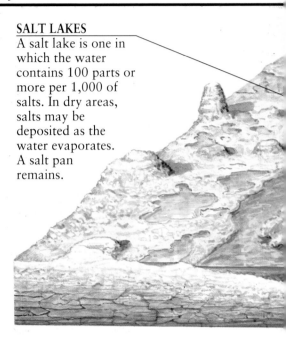

SALT LAKES
A salt lake is one in which the water contains 100 parts or more per 1,000 of salts. In dry areas, salts may be deposited as the water evaporates. A salt pan remains.

THE BAHAMAS
In the warm, shallow seas around the Bahamas, oolitic limestones are being formed today. Lime comes out of solution and builds up around other tiny grains of lime.

LOOK OUT FOR THESE

OOLITE
The grains of oolite, or oolitic limestone, look like fish eggs held together by a cement of lime.

LIMESTONE
Limestone may build up from fossil and shell fragments. It may contain whole or broken fossils.

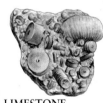

DOLOMITE
This is a type of limestone that contains a lot of the mineral called dolomite.

FLINT
A flint nodule usually has a whitish outer layer. When broken open, the flint is grayish or almost black in color.

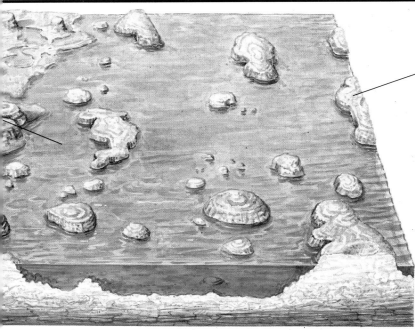

FIRST OUT

As the water evaporates, those salts that are least easily dissolved are deposited first. Lime is one of the first to appear, as is magnesium carbonate, followed by gypsum and anhydrite.

IN THE CENTER

If an area of seawater dries up, common salt and magnesium sulfate are deposited. Salt pans in sheltered lagoons are often an important source of rock salt.

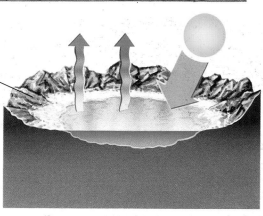

IRONSTONE

Ironstone is a rock that contains at least 15 percent of iron minerals, such as siderite.

ROCK SALT

Rock salt is colorless or white, but it may be tinted by other minerals. It is made mainly of sodium chloride.

ROCK GYPSUM

This is composed of calcium sulfate. It is formed when water evaporates and leaves a deposit.

PHOSPHATE ROCK

This is made from chemicals, called phosphates, of iron, calcium, and aluminum.

Coal, Oil, and Gas

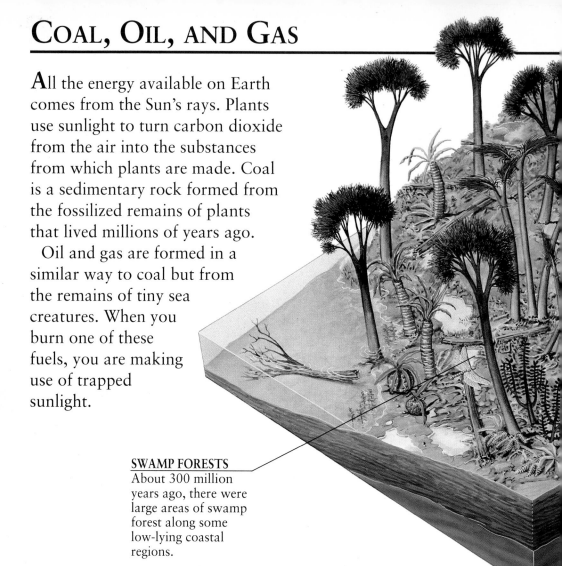

All the energy available on Earth comes from the Sun's rays. Plants use sunlight to turn carbon dioxide from the air into the substances from which plants are made. Coal is a sedimentary rock formed from the fossilized remains of plants that lived millions of years ago.

Oil and gas are formed in a similar way to coal but from the remains of tiny sea creatures. When you burn one of these fuels, you are making use of trapped sunlight.

SWAMP FORESTS
About 300 million years ago, there were large areas of swamp forest along some low-lying coastal regions.

LOOK OUT FOR THESE

PEAT
Peat is a black soil formed from plant remains that decayed in boggy areas where there was little air. When dry, peat can be burned as fuel.

BROWN COAL
This is a soft, dull-looking, earthy type of coal. Some types burn well and give out quite a lot of heat.

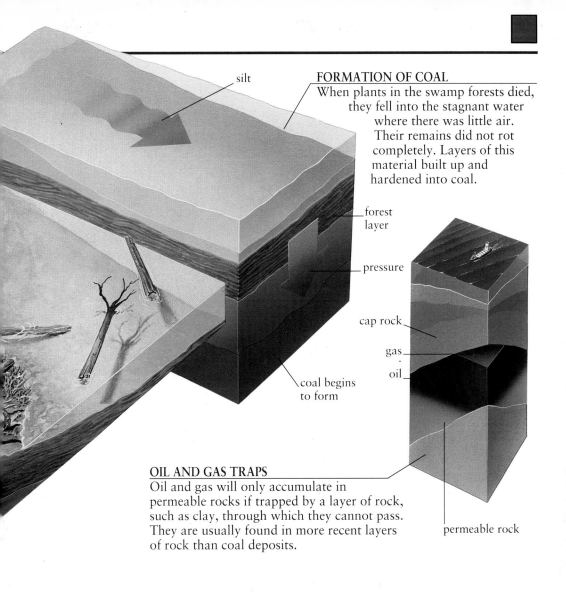

silt

FORMATION OF COAL
When plants in the swamp forests died, they fell into the stagnant water where there was little air. Their remains did not rot completely. Layers of this material built up and hardened into coal.

forest layer

pressure

cap rock

gas

oil

coal begins to form

OIL AND GAS TRAPS
Oil and gas will only accumulate in permeable rocks if trapped by a layer of rock, such as clay, through which they cannot pass. They are usually found in more recent layers of rock than coal deposits.

permeable rock

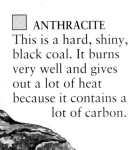

■ ANTHRACITE
This is a hard, shiny, black coal. It burns very well and gives out a lot of heat because it contains a lot of carbon.

Lepidodendron

Neuropteris

Annularia

■ FOSSIL PLANTS
Coal is one of the best rocks in which to find fossil plants. You might see impressions of stems, leaves, or even whole plants.

ROCKS CHANGED BY HEAT

When hot igneous magma is thrust up through the layers of the crust into the surrounding rocks, it bakes the rocks surrounding it. As the heat spreads out from the igneous rock, it changes the rocks around it. The minerals in the rocks recrystallize and form new types of rock. This is called contact or thermal metamorphism. Typical rocks that are formed in this way are hornfels and skarn.

COUNTRY ROCKS
The rocks around an igneous intrusion are often called country rocks.

IGNEOUS INTRUSION
The hot igneous rock that is forced into surrounding rocks is called an igneous intrusion. The bigger it is, the more heat it contains. And it is the amount of heat that causes the rocks to change.

 **LOOK OUT FOR THESE**

SPOTTED SLATE
This rock may vary in color from gray or green to purple and black. It has darker spots. It is formed on the outside of a metamorphic aureole.

HORNFELS
A hornfels is a hard rock that varies in color from green to black. It is found on the inner side of the aureole, where the heat was greatest.

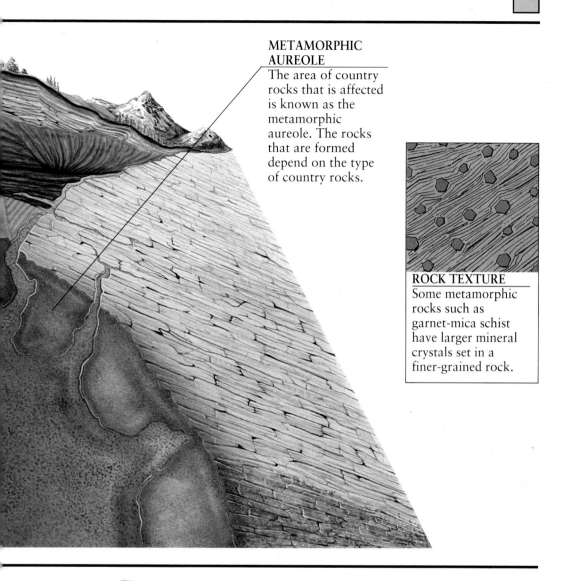

METAMORPHIC AUREOLE

The area of country rocks that is affected is known as the metamorphic aureole. The rocks that are formed depend on the type of country rocks.

ROCK TEXTURE

Some metamorphic rocks such as garnet-mica schist have larger mineral crystals set in a finer-grained rock.

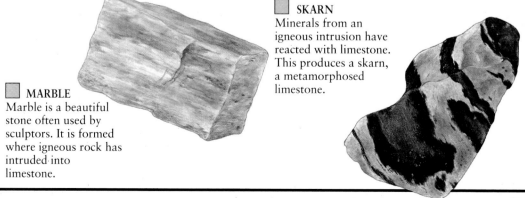

MARBLE

Marble is a beautiful stone often used by sculptors. It is formed where igneous rock has intruded into limestone.

SKARN

Minerals from an igneous intrusion have reacted with limestone. This produces a skarn, a metamorphosed limestone.

ROCKS CHANGED BY HEAT AND PRESSURE

Scientists believe that the outer layer of the earth, the crust and upper mantle, is made up of a series of rigid plates. These plates are moving very slowly in relation to one another. So this outer skin is rather like a slow-motion, floating, global jigsaw. Where a plate of continental crust collides with a plate of oceanic crust, lines of weakness occur and volcanoes erupt, fed by magma from the mantle below. Layers of sedimentary rocks carried by the plates are also crumpled and folded to form new mountain ranges.

HOW THE ROCKS ARE AFFECTED
During mountain building, the rocks are changed by heat from the igneous activity and also by pressure.

BANDED GNEISS
It is sometimes easy to identify an outcrop of rock as metamorphic. This banded rock has been intensely metamorphosed.

 **LOOK OUT FOR THESE**

SLATE
Slate is often used for roofing and pool tables. This is because it can be cleaved (split) into perfectly flat sheets with a smooth surface.

PHYLLITE
This rock is often greenish or gray in color. Like slate, it will cleave into sheets and then the surface has a silvery sheen.

SCHIST
Schist also has a layered texture. But the layers may be crumpled and may glisten with flakes of mica.

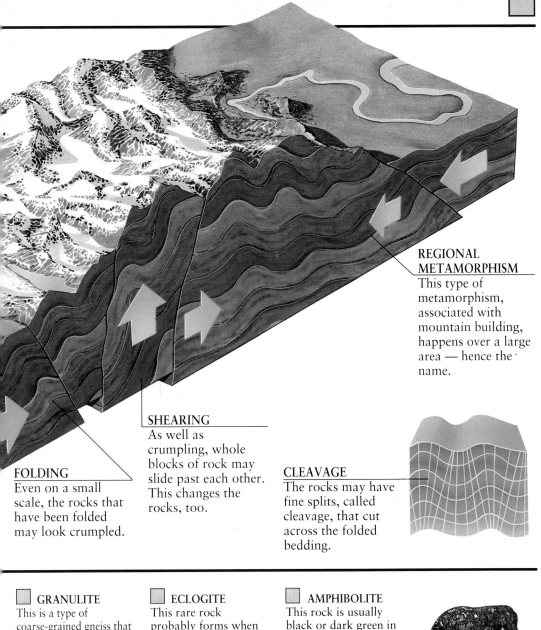

REGIONAL METAMORPHISM

This type of metamorphism, associated with mountain building, happens over a large area — hence the name.

SHEARING

As well as crumpling, whole blocks of rock may slide past each other. This changes the rocks, too.

FOLDING

Even on a small scale, the rocks that have been folded may look crumpled.

CLEAVAGE

The rocks may have fine splits, called cleavage, that cut across the folded bedding.

■ GRANULITE

This is a type of coarse-grained gneiss that has been metamorphosed deep in the earth's crust.

■ ECLOGITE

This rare rock probably forms when basalt is subjected to high pressures and temperatures in the mantle.

■ AMPHIBOLITE

This rock is usually black or dark green in color. It is formed by the metamorphism of igneous rocks, such as basalt.

LIMESTONE SCENERY

Calcite, or calcium carbonate, which forms at least half of the mineral content of limestone, will dissolve in slightly acid water. Rainwater is acid because it dissolves carbon dioxide from the air to form weak carbonic acid. Because limestone — and dolomite — can be dissolved by rainwater, a distinctive kind of landscape develops where these rocks are present.

KARST SCENERY
Landscape changed and shaped by a solution of limestone develops sagging surfaces, sinkholes, and areas of collapse. Such landscapes are called karst areas after an area in eastern Europe.

WIDENING THE GAP
By dissolving the limestone, rainwater will widen any cracks or joints in the rock.

UNDERGROUND RIVERS
Where joints and bedding planes are enlarged, large streams can vanish underground.

LOOK OUT FOR THESE

 **LIMESTONE PAVEMENT**
Limestone pavements consist of large blocks cut by gutters.

 **SINKHOLE**
A steep-sided shaft in a limestone area is called a sinkhole or doline.

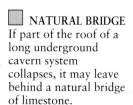 **NATURAL BRIDGE**
If part of the roof of a long underground cavern system collapses, it may leave behind a natural bridge of limestone.

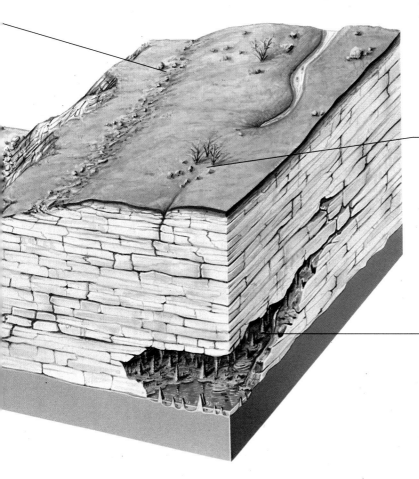

NATURAL SHAFT

Where joints in limestone cross, water may run down the gaps and dissolve away limestone so that a deep hole is formed.

CAVES AND CAVERNS

An underground stream may create a cavern system. Stalactites, formed by the evaporation of lime from dripping water, may hang from the roof and stalagmites grow up from the floor.

☐ LIMESTONE GORGE

If there is no bridge left behind, or if the bridge collapses, a deep gorge remains, cutting through the landscape.

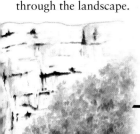

☐ PETRIFYING SPRING

A stream may emerge as a spring at the edge of the limestone. Lime is dissolved in the water. It may coat objects and form limestone rock deposits. This type of rock is known as tufa.

SEDIMENTS AND FOSSILS

As layers of sediment grow thicker, the weight tends to pack the grains beneath even closer. Water rich in minerals percolates among the grains of sediment, leaving behind a kind of cement. In this way, soft sediments are turned into hard rocks. If an animal or plant dies and its body is buried in sediment, parts of it may be preserved over millions of years as part of the rock.

AN ANIMAL OR PLANT DIES

When an animal, like this marine reptile, an ichthyosaur, dies, its body falls to the seabed and its flesh will rot away.

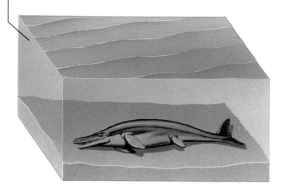

THE FOSSIL RECORD

Fossils can help to tell the age of a rock.

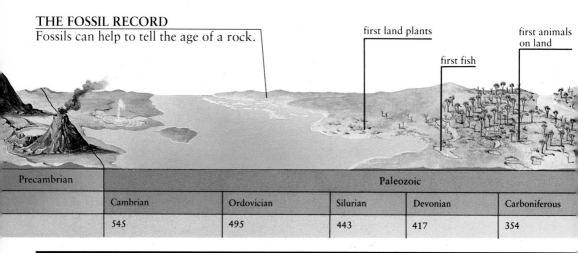

first land plants

first fish

first animals on land

Precambrian	Paleozoic				
	Cambrian	Ordovician	Silurian	Devonian	Carboniferous
	545	495	443	417	354

✓ LOOK OUT FOR THESE

☐ REPLACEMENT

The original fossil may be dissolved away. At the same time, another mineral may replace it.

☐ MOLD

The impression of a fossil in the rock in which it was formed is called a mold.

☐ CAST

If a mold is later filled with new material, this fossillike object is called a cast.

☐ ECHINOID

This creature is similar to the sand dollar that lives in the sea today. The fossil is very common, especially in chalk.

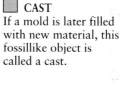

FOSSILIZATION

If they are not broken up, the bones may become buried in sediments that then harden into rock.

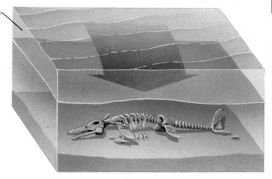

DISCOVERY

When the rocks are exposed, perhaps millions of years later, the remains of the animal may be discovered as a fossil.

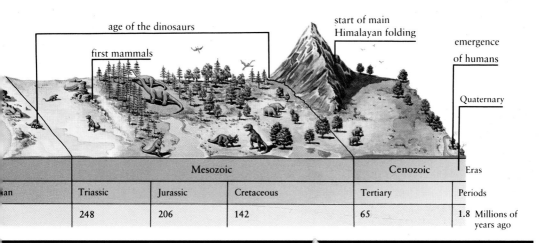

age of the dinosaurs

first mammals

start of main
Himalayan folding

emergence
of humans

Quaternary

	Mesozoic			Cenozoic		Eras
...an	Triassic	Jurassic	Cretaceous	Tertiary		Periods
	248	206	142	65	1.8	Millions of years ago

AMMONITE
Ammonites, looking somewhat like stony rams' horns, are very common fossils.

TRILOBITE
These animals were related to insects and wood lice but they foraged for food near the seabed.

SHARK'S TOOTH
The skeleton of a shark is not made of bone but of cartilage. However, its teeth are very hard and are often preserved as fossils.

INSECTS IN AMBER
Sticky sap running down a tree may trap an insect. The sap may then harden into amber.

37

NATIVE ELEMENTS AND GEMSTONES

A native element occurs in nature uncombined with any other element as a mineral. Some valuable metals, such as gold and silver, occur like this. Sulfur can appear as crystals or as crusts around volcanoes. Carbon can occur as a native element in the form of graphite or as diamonds. Diamonds are prized for their hardness and their beauty, especially when cut, and so they are regarded as gemstones.

DIAMOND RING
Most gem-quality diamonds, such as this one, are very small. The largest diamond ever found weighed more than 1 pound (0.5 kilogram).

PANNING FOR GOLD
A traditional way of looking for gold is by panning. Gravel that might contain gold was swirled around in a large pan with water. Panning is still used in some countries to search for metals.

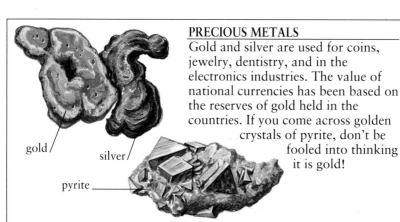

PRECIOUS METALS
Gold and silver are used for coins, jewelry, dentistry, and in the electronics industries. The value of national currencies has been based on the reserves of gold held in the countries. If you come across golden crystals of pyrite, don't be fooled into thinking it is gold!

gold

silver

pyrite

LOOK OUT FOR THESE

DIAMOND
Diamond is the hardest naturally occurring substance. It is chemically the same as the graphite in a "lead" pencil. Most diamonds come from South Africa, Russia, Namibia, and Australia.

OPAL
Opal is a form of silica. It is actually a solidified gel so it does not occur in crystals. It has a lovely glassy sheen.

HEAVY METAL
Gold is heavier than
silt or gravel and is
left behind when all
the lighter material
has been washed
away.

SAPPHIRE
Like ruby, sapphire is a
gemstone form of the
mineral corundum.
The blue color may
vary from almost
colorless to very dark.

PEARL
Not strictly a gemstone,
pearl is made from a
substance that an oyster
produces when grit
enters its shell.

TURQUOISE
Turquoise is usually
found as masses, and
crystals are rare. It is
prized for its color
and sheen when
polished.

AMETHYST
Amethyst is a form of
quartz. Because of its
lovely purple color, it
is regarded as a semi-
precious stone.

ROCKS AND MINERALS AT WORK

Rocks and minerals are vital to our everyday lives. Buildings are constructed from stone, rock products, or brick — and brick is made partly from clay. Important chemicals, such as sulfur, can be extracted directly from the earth. Natural ores containing important metals, such as iron and aluminum, are sometimes mined in vast open quarries. Here the ore is often broken up by explosives and then carried away to be heated (smelted) at high temperatures to extract the metals. Today's technology depends on the silicon chip; silicon comes from quartz.

STRIP MINE

To get at ores, coal, minerals, or even kaolin (a white clay), the surface soil and rock are stripped away. This is called strip or opencast mining. It has been used for centuries.

SHAFT MINING

To get at coal or minerals at great depths, a vertical shaft is dug. From the shaft, miners bore horizontal tunnels.

BIG DIGGERS

Huge machines can scrape away the rock ready for loading on to trucks.

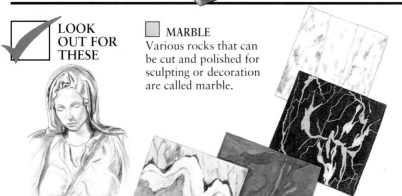

LOOK OUT FOR THESE

MARBLE

Various rocks that can be cut and polished for sculpting or decoration are called marble.

FLINT AX

Humans have been using flint tools for at least 70,000 years. At first, tools were just flakes of stone.

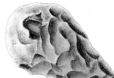

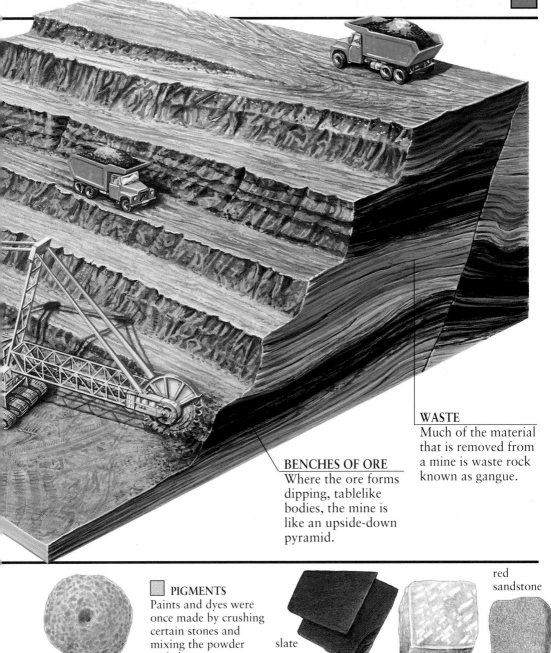

WASTE
Much of the material
that is removed from
a mine is waste rock
known as gangue.

BENCHES OF ORE
Where the ore forms
dipping, tablelike
bodies, the mine is
like an upside-down
pyramid.

PIGMENTS
Paints and dyes were
once made by crushing
certain stones and
mixing the powder
with fat.

slate

red
sandstone

limestone

GRINDING STONE
Even today, grinding
stones are still used to
grind wheat and other
cereals into flour.

**BUILDING
STONES**
Here are four types of
rock that are
commonly used for
building and roofing.

oolitic
limestone

COLLECTING ROCKS AND FOSSILS

You can learn a lot about Earth and the history of the landscape by collecting rocks and minerals. It is also fun to display them properly. Most local and national museums have collections of rocks and minerals on display. They will also have books on sites of geological interest as well as information on clubs to join. Remember, collectors who are not careful can damage the countryside and cause serious injury. All quarries are owned by someone, and old quarries can be dangerous places. **Never** enter one on your own or without permission.

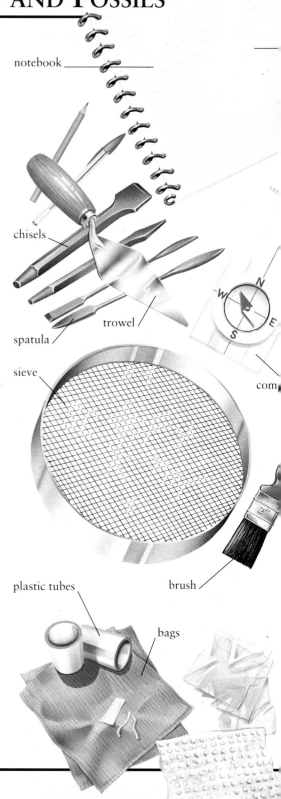

notebook

chisels

trowel

spatula

sieve

com

brush

plastic tubes

bags

DISPLAYING YOUR FINDS
Keep each specimen in a separate labeled tray or shelf. You can buy special collecting cabinets with shallow drawers, but perhaps you could make something just as suitable.

MAKING A RECORD

You need just a simple notebook to record the details of your find. Number your record and the specimen. A photograph or sketch of the location is valuable.

SAFETY GEAR

You should **always** wear a hard hat, sturdy gloves, and safety goggles.

PACKING YOUR FINDS

Wrap each specimen in newspaper. Pack delicate crystals in a box or tube. You will need a comfortable knapsack to carry your finds and your equipment.

TOOLS FOR THE JOB

Use a real geologist's hammer. Other kinds can splinter and the sharp fragments are dangerous. You will need some chisels, a magnifying glass, and one or two other items.

map

PLANNING A TRIP

Large-scale maps, geological maps, and guidebooks will help you decide where to go. It is useful to learn how to use a compass properly.

43

GLOSSARY

Words in SMALL CAPITAL letters indicate a cross-reference.

atmosphere The layer of air that surrounds Earth.

atom The smallest unit of an ELEMENT. The atoms of each element have the same number of PROTONS and ELECTRONS.

bed A sheetlike layer of SEDIMENTARY ROCK.

bedding plane The surface between one BED and another.

breccia SEDIMENTARY ROCK made up of large angular grains.

carbon dioxide One of the gases that occurs naturally in the ATMOSPHERE. It is a COMPOUND of the ELEMENTS carbon and oxygen.

compound A combination of more than one ELEMENT.

core The dense center part of the earth made up of an inner and an outer core and consisting mostly of nickel and iron.

crust The thin, rocky outer layer of the earth.

crust, continental CRUST that occurs under the continents. It is made of a granitelike material and varies from 18.6 to 43.4 miles (30 to 70 kilometers) thick.

crust, oceanic CRUST that occurs under the ocean bed. It is made of basaltlike material and is about 3 miles (5 kilometers) thick.

crystal A solid that occurs naturally. It has a definite chemical composition and structure and shows SYMMETRY.

current A flow, as a river does or as may occur in the sea.

delta A flat plain of sediment deposited in the shape of a triangle.

dinosaur Any of the extinct, sometimes gigantic, REPTILES that lived during Mesozoic times.

earthquake A movement within the earth that sends out shock waves.

electron One of the particles from which ATOMS are made. It carries a tiny negative electrical charge.

element Any of the substances, such as gold or sulfur, made up from ATOMS that all have the same number of PROTONS. These are the "building blocks" of matter.

fold A physical structure in which the beds of rock are bent or curved.

fossil Any trace or remains, preserved in the ROCKS, of an animal or plant that was once alive. Fossils are used to calculate the age of a rock.

galaxy Any system of STARS held together by GRAVITY.

gel A jellylike material in which solid particles are dispersed in liquid.

gem A MINERAL that is prized for its beauty.

glacier A large mass of ice that moves very slowly.

glass A solid that has turned from a liquid to a solid so quickly that CRYSTALS have not had time to form.

granite A common, coarse-grained IGNEOUS ROCK, consisting of quartz, mica, and feldspars.

gravity The force of attraction that all objects have for one another. On Earth, all objects tend to fall toward the center of the planet.

ice age A period in Earth's history when large sheets of ice spread outward from the poles. The last ice age finished around 15,000 years ago.

igneous rock A ROCK that has formed from a cooling MAGMA.

intrusion A body of IGNEOUS ROCK that has been thrust into other rocks.

lava Molten, or melted, ROCK material that flows from a VOLCANO.

limestone A SEDIMENTARY ROCK mainly made up of calcite from fossils and shell fragments.

magma Molten ROCK at high temperature and pressure from the earth's MANTLE. IGNEOUS ROCKS are formed from magma.

mantle The hot, rocky layer of the earth between the CORE and the CRUST. MAGMA comes from the mantle.

massive Lacking CRYSTAL form.

metamorphic rock A ROCK that has formed as other rocks have been subjected to heat and/or pressure: a "changed" rock.

mineral A naturally occurring substance with a definite chemical composition and a CRYSTAL structure.

ore A ROCK or MINERAL that contains a metal that can be extracted, often by strip mining.

permeable A term used to describe ROCKS that contain pores through which liquid, such as water or oil, can pass.

proton One of the particles from which ATOMS are made. It carries a tiny positive electrical charge.

reptile Any of the cold-blooded, backboned animals, such as a snake or lizard, that are adapted to living on land and that usually lay eggs with a leathery shell.

rock A naturally occurring mass of MINERALS.

sedimentary rock A ROCK, such as sandstone, composed of particles of other rocks.

seismometer An instrument used to detect and record the shock waves from EARTHQUAKES.

soil The loose mixture of ROCK and animal and plant debris that lies above solid ROCK.

star Any of the bodies in space that radiate energy generated from itself. Our Sun is a star.

symmetry The regularity of the shape of a CRYSTAL. The symmetry reflects the arrangement of the crystal's ATOMS.

texture The sizes, shapes, and arrangements of particles in a ROCK.

tide The regular rising and falling of the oceans in response to the pull of gravity of the sun and especially the moon.

volcano A tear in the earth's CRUST through which LAVA, gas, ash, and other material flow out to the surface.

INDEX